Poems from Planet P

You are Here

Portland, Ore.

Jennifer M. Fulford

Black Bomb Books
Asheville, NC
www.BlackBombBooks.com
blackbombbooks@gmail.com

Copyright © 2015 Jennifer M. Fulford

First Edition, March 2015

All rights reserved. No part of this publication may be reproduced, distributed, or transmitted in any form or by any means, including photocopying, recording or other electronic or mechanical methods, without prior permission of the publishers, except in the case of brief quotations embodied in critical reviews and certain other noncommercial uses permitted by copyright laws. For permission requests, contact the publisher.

Cover design by Kate Irwin, kateink.com
Cover background from Jet Propulsion Labs, NASA
Cover photo of rose by Jennifer M. Fulford
Author photo by Camille Rantis

ISBN: 978-0692391716

*For Lady, my Golden Retriever,
who never questioned a single line.*

CONTENTS

1 Poems About Poetry
    Emily D and Me, 4
    Infatuation in Ink, 5
    A Poet's Stick, 6
    Poetic Advice from The Attic, 7
    Even Poets Suffer Typos, 8
    Poets are Riff-Raff, 9
    Who Dares, 10
    It Came in the Night, 11

2 Poems About Lament
    The Gadget Store on a Sunday Afternoon, 14
    Why We Must Not Drop the Bomb Again, 15
    Sara Last-Initial, 16
    I Swapped a '74 Mustang for This, 17
    That Part of Me, 18

3 Poems About Beauty
    Sex on a Bike, 20
    Kernel of Salty Honey, 21
    I Am, 22
    The Tyranny of Choice, 23
    Women, You Should, 24

4 Poems of the Bizarre
    Poem for Planet P, 26
    Yams on Salmon St., 27
    Opinion of the Bulldog in a Zippered Fleece, 28
    Meditation on *Dog is My Co-Pilot,* 29-30

Inducement

BUY NOW. INCREASE YOUR CREATIVITY. FOR A LIMITED TIME ONLY. 100 PERCENT SATISFACTION GUARANTEED. NO GIMMICKS. IMPRESS YOUR FRIENDS AND CO-WORKERS. JUMP START YOUR CAREER. LITTLE OR NOTHING DOWN. RESULTS IN DAYS. WORKS WONDERS. TRAIN SMALL DOGS IN HOURS. MONEY-BACK IF NOT COMPLETELY SATISFIED. TESTED BY MILLIONS. WORK FROM HOME. NO COLD CALLS. NO EXPERIENCE NECESSARY. NO ID REQUIRED. LEARN FROM THE EXPERTS. SEE THE SEVEN WONDERS OF THE WORLD. MAKE MONEY IN NO TIME. TOLL FREE. BE AN INSTANT PRO. LIVE THE LIFE YOU'VE ALWAYS WANTED. FIND NIRVANA. MEET YOUR MATCH. MEET YOUR MAKER. FOSTER WORLD PEACE. RIGHT HERE. RIGHT NOW. BEFORE IT'S TOO LATE.

1
Poems About Poetry

Emily D and Me

I wanted to write a poem about Emily Dickinson
        suffering through a 12-step program.

If she shared, she might confess:
        "Hello, I'm Emily D and I'm a word-aholic.
        I retreated from life to sip the elixir of poetry.
        I am conflicted by my pen and defeated by love.
        My heart grows giant and my mind closes round.
        I reject the real world for the abstract.
        I drink ink for the high of perfect phrasing."

My attempt to write her a poem suffered melancholy.
        I paced the floorboards a few weeks.
        Underneath, she knocked like Poe's heart.
        A rap song might suffice, but she was not interested.
        When humidity fogged my panes, my finger drew words
        in the dew. The lines ran together.
        She stalked me from room to car to Mt. Tabor dog park.
        Behind me, she prodded - *take my words along, if not me*.
        And some 1500 notions later, my efforts at her capture
        led me to drink.

Far more expert at indulgence, she mocked my idolatry.
        She flaunted her ink-stained fingers.
        She knitted her brow and half-smiled.
        She tightened her legs and her bun.
        This superior wren with tragic vision,
        too drunk from copious consumption,
        never realized her own genius.

Infatuation in Ink

I read the best of the best today,
living poets.

Their words couple and are coupling,
cerebral copulation.

The beauty of their meter stings my eyes,
jealous voyeurism.

Side by side, we spoon, warm teacher,
naked amateur.

Where I whisper across the neckline,
take me.

A Poet's Stick

Dare poetry be silliness?
Fractured and vociferous?
On good terms with bad flatulence?
Why does the world keep spinning us?

In Powell's, a stand-up poet once,
who lived by choice in homelessness,
captured each particulate
of his enraptured audience.

He aimed his words and shook the room,
deriding bombs and guns and doom,
slamming war as a useless tool,
"Let verse combat our history."

He blasted, "NO we should not trust
the lords of war, their pleas to crush."
The message clear, pointing at us:
"Silence breeds ugly outcomes."

The pacing man-boy drew applause.
He never smiled, body faint and long.
Stick-thin, white skin, incomplete, and flawed.
His kingdom -- rhyme and tenor.

Dare poetry be silliness?
Fractured and vociferous?
On good terms with bad flatulence?
Why does the world keep spinning us?

Poetic Advice from The Attic

The poet shakes the dust from his sleeve and sees genius.
    Countless particles. Years of shed skin. Proof of dues paid.

His words thicken the room and tighten the novice's airway,
    like cotton and castor oil.

His advice enters the lungs, bloats and constricts,
    so there's no arguing around it. Resistance depletes the air.

He declares the coughing your problem.

Even Poets Suffer Typos

Darn the needles, crack the peanuts,
I blame my lot on screwy syntax,
scary prospects for the untested,
a faux-et whom no one's invested.

So I can't spell or use a colon,
semi-awful full of run-ons.
Find a hat trick in my spell check.
Erase the offense with a quick click.

Lick a stamp and send it somewhere
where the editors scoff and slumber
atop piles of other verses
drooling o'er the greenhorn's curses:

Did I send it with a typo!?
Damn the jitters and the pinot.

A complete joker, I need a smoke now.
I don't smoke, just hand me choco-
covered ego, nuts, and Ho Hos
'til I climb out of this hell hole.

Poets are Riff-Raff

I don't care for the poets I don't "get."
The BS is thick. Us common folk
won't take the time to understand.

My anti-intellectual class wants burgers 'n guns 'n idols
like their outlaw in-laws who take over TV reality shows
and cat-call the President.

Who cares if I write a poem
worthy of a blogpost,
or an anthology book,
or a coffeehouse nook
amongst a sea of MacBooks
at Albina's lounge for slackers.

Just give me the coffee, for Christ's sake,
you over-educated uppity barista behind the counter, you,
and I'll read the poem in *The New Yorker*, page 52,
and snivel.

That one, *I got.*

Who Dares

Who so much as dares to write a word
when all the world is filled with tongues

And thought is but a word kept in
from the tower of simpering sorrows and wrongs

Oh, lost ideas gust
through the inner grass

The places of *shhh* and imaginings
Thrash

The words, written,
seem weak and obtuse

The *ahh* or the *mmm*
speak louder than truth

Listen close in
the mind whispers and moans

The sound, within,
finds meaning, atoned

It Came in the Night

The dishes will toast.

The dust bunnies will mingle.

The socks will eat their young.

The beds will make whoopie.

The laundry will pucker.

The vacuum will sulk.

Let them.

The words are hungry.

2
Poems About Lament

The Gadget Store on a Sunday Afternoon

The buyers belly-up to the teak at the cell phone store
in Pioneer Place on Sabbath,
like legions of Sudanese clawing for a bite to eat.

From my pocket, I could tweet the truth
while I upgrade my identity.
My phone, my right, my God-given liberty to speak.

The freedom I hold in my hand holds the world,
designed to make me wiser, an easy tap away,
yet I am not wise.

The new gadget promises wisdom, light years faster,
but my master just the same.
A flat glow, it hypnotizes me from another world,
where my junk ends, the real mirage, a mercury bed,
a land of feet and hands, a minefield of survival.

Why We Must Not Drop the Bomb Again

Stored in these shoes is someone's love,
sewn together by small hands for unknown wages.
She fits my feet with aching conscience.

She'll spend her coins on eggs or rice or an ounce of meat
to feed her child or children in an inconsequential place.

The distance to us silences her voice.
Men who make nothing control everything,
      no drum beating for change.

She reaches for tender moments, a chicken bone for stock,
feathers for a pallet, small scraps to the world at large.
Here, we declare the collateral damage worth the shoes.

Sara Last-Initial

The patient who looked like the Girl with the Dragon Tattoo
    reeked of cigarettes.

The smell triggered a remembrance of my cousins
    who, for breakfast, drank Dr. Pepper
    from refundable glass bottles.

The girl, kept neat, was gray mood and pale and shaky as hell
    underneath emo clothes
    that made her perfect teeth whiter.

She used "like" and "yeah" but glowed with Cover Girl Goth appeal,
    her darkly painted eyes repelled no one
    and attracted everyone.

She wore size 8 shoes and leggings with holes the first day,
    and tie-dye, the next.
    Her graphic tee said something loud.

Her hair slanted over one eye and obscured her pretty stare,
    maybe a warning.
    Turn the other way but
    she could bum a smoke in an easy second.

She wouldn't eat lentils for fear they'd have worms,
    never did her psyche-prescribed homework for group,
    and kept neat.

She admitted doing mushrooms the night before.
    No judgment here in group
    just nods and blinks to her "likes" and "yeahs."

I wanted her teeth, her fresh teenage neurosis
    to replace my worn-out 20-year soundtrack of complaint,
    outdated music to hers.

I Swapped a '74 Mustang for This

I rev the engine of the men I knew back then,
   a distant cruise on a town square in Missouri,
   where youth and recklessness once thrived.

Time dubs over the places young hands roamed
   as my tires squeal near the end of the road up ahead,
   and my hands clutch the wheel of time at a sharp curve.

The foolish rides I took sometimes roar over the exhaust of age.
   They spark when my tank's half empty,
   and I'm broken down again.

Cassettes, brown tape, distort in glove boxes of memories.
   The ghosts are streetlights and people,
   too much beer, Calvin Kleins, and the pill.

At sundown, the cheap thrills resurface,
   forgotten songs unwind from an old frequency inside my head,
   to sustain me a year or two longer.

                  --for Rebecca

That Part of Me

That part of me that dislikes sorting socks.
That part of me that leaves messes in the sink.
That part of me that lets it all pile up.
That part of me that knows my mother disapproves.
That part of me that doesn't care.
That part of me that is old enough to do it my way.
That part of me that thinks about running naked in the park.
That part of me that almost did.
That part of me that recalls that warm night on the jungle gym.
That part of me that wonders what happened to him.
That part of me that still asks around.
That part of me that likes that naughty part of me.
That part of me that wants to drive a motorcycle.
That part of me that needs to race it through Paris.
That part of me that will never have enough money.
That part of me that feels like time is running out.
That part of me that is looking old.
That part of me that needs to get over it.
That part of me that <u>fill in the blank</u>.
That part of me that loses her train of thought.
That part of me that regrets that foolish love letter.
That part of me that knows she'd probably write it again.
That part of me that should have memorized it.
That part of me that thinks being sentimental is crap.
That part of me that rarely learns from her patterns.
That part of me that refuses to go deep.
That part of me that ignores that empty part of me.
That part of me that is sure that doesn't matter.
That part of me that loves the word *that*.
That part of me that can't be described by a poem about that part of me.

3
Poems About Beauty

Sex on a Bike

The whir of the chain
glides him close.
He inhales more air,
pavement, vibration.

He pumps up hill,
through the night,
and thrums with life
into our shared darkness.

His body gyrates.
Legs and hips slip to and fro,
'til he alights on my skin
and triggers a song for the groove.

Kernel of Salty Honey

May I give you a gem?
That's not out of place?
Or meant for your ring finger?

If you set aside my gift,
how would I feel?
Dusty.

It collects cobwebs
on your dresser,
next to your wedding ring.

The gold you put on each day
for the one you kiss each night.
Familiar.

Ordinariness is tangible to the touch
rather than the salty honey of a flung-off
line of poetry in a book you'll never read.

My gem -- my words -- lack realness.
They can't make toast or coffee.
Fleeting.

Real is a person
by your side, in your bed
filling your hand with hers.

I Am

For I am the finite.
For I am the wonder.
For I am the cloud in the corner
      the trembling sky
      the cluster of gray.

For I am the roiling.
For I am the thunder.
For I am the flash of filament
      the spark of comets
      the stardust way.

For I am the mystery.
For I am the sojourner.
For I am the answer
      the dawn of knowing
      the light of day.

The Tyranny of Choice

Paper or plastic or canvas or compostable microfiber
Yogurt in tubs or gallons or swirled or with crumbles
Bread made of wheat, white, potato, oatmeal or seeds
Shoes named Vans or Sketchers or superstars, no laces
Cars called third world countries or creatures, probably extinct
Nail polish in neon, same as movies or hair dyes or novels

(God bless the dreamers)

Wash the merch down with microbrewed pilsner
or wine mixed with chocolate
or mixologist whiskey
or java-soaked ale

I want simple
Sunlight
Dawn
Awe
Laughs
True love
I want complex

or a wonder-led life
or a people unsuffering
or sleepless nights of creation
Wash the intangibles down with bitter humility

(God bless the dreamers)

Words in good books or a poem that squeezes or an urge to make love
Thoughts that demand pens or bliss to be spoken or kiss to be taken
Emotions that trim wrinkles or replace burnt bridges or run off in song
Longings of the ages, pondered or buried, the answers no closer
Good stories or old pictures or yellow letters or memories, forgotten
Kindreds who challenge or listen or forgive the missteps, the many

Women, You Should

Wing it and never worry later.
Glenn Beck doesn't care
before he opens his mouth
and reaps millions, stuffed in,
spewing ego-bloated falsehoods
and hate and absurdities.

TV glorifies fake gods.
Fox creates horse's asses.
So women, move up.
Take control of your voices
and reclaim your infamous genesis
before the rapture begins.

4
Poems of the Bizarre

Poem for Planet P

Neither Portland nor Pluto
        earns planethood.
Just a hemisphere of DNA,
        a scrap of solar dust
        inside my ear.
Not quite revered,
        each heavenly body a renegade,
        an asteroid, a tumbling rock,
        where rules defy Newton's gravity.
Whether by relation or imagination,
        the two deserve each other's company.

Yams on Salmon St.

Tell a guest you melted marshmallows on the sweet potatoes and expect the worst.

Guest One: *The spongy white confection is housemates with Jello, and Miracle Whip and Kool-Aid!*

Guest Two: *A marshmallow is fabricated dough, a cartoon Stay Puft Man in a sailor suit!*

Guest Three: *To suggest it will dignify an age-old powerfood borders on heresy!*

Last Guest: *Less than pure, it's culinary tragedy!*

Opinion of the Bulldog in a Zippered Fleece

As I sadly saunter,
        rock on my haunch and ponder,
a frightful parade, I wander,
        in a zipper and a collar,
bought on sale for just a dollar.
        My dignity surely squandered.

Meditation on *Dog is My Co-Pilot*

This universe is small enough to write to my creator. Dog.

She/he/id/*ohm,* a benevolent furry savior,
a nuzzle, a lick, a steady paw on the emergency stick
to slow our spiral into the ravine.

My dog's glance advises me: 'You're on your own.'
'Smoke 'em if you got 'em.'
'Fur is cheap and so are bumper stickers.'

My first draft of God/Dog was silliness (see Footnote #1)
scribbled on the back of a paper scrap
hastily rummaged from the recycling bin
at the postage place/weigh station/point-of-all-outgoing light. (see Footnote #2)

The scrap letter read: *So leave the worldly thoughts behind
and find the truth that is for you within yourself at this time.
You're all messengers the same as I.* (see Footnote #3)

My creator panted the entire time.

Footnotes

Footnote #1: My first silly verse about the bumper sticker *Dog is My Co-Pilot* spotted near Stark Street went like this:

> Crazy, crazy as a loon,
> Suck a helium balloon.
> Ratchet, gadget, crank and croon,
> God/Dog boomerang the moon.

Footnote #2: The UPS Store on Hawthorne Boulevard, one of my favorite places in Portland, Ore.

Footnote #3: I really did retrieve a tossed-out religious letter from the recycling bin at the UPS store. It channeled a message from Jesus. It was one page, single-spaced, unsigned, and obviously typed on a manual typewriter. I was desperate for a piece of paper to write down Footnote #1.

Acknowledgments

The following take no responsibility for assisting this collection but earn my high regard:

- ❖ Sally Lehman, my most steadfast writer pal and sounding board.
- ❖ Pattie Palmer Baker, whose poetry deserves greater attention.
- ❖ Judith Pulman, a gem of an advisor and word comrade.
- ❖ Ava and Stephen Collopy, my secret inspirations.
- ❖ Bonnie Ditlevsen, super agent for the open mic.
- ❖ Doug Storm, who humors me and calls me out.
- ❖ Multnomah Arts Center, dedicated to affordable arts education.
- ❖ The Poetry Group at Wy'East UU Congregation, lovers of poems.
- ❖ VoiceCatcher, for its vision to strengthening women writers.
- ❖ Willamette Writers, supporters of all intrepid writing souls.
- ❖ Cece Rantis, who models great ease in creative ventures.
- ❖ Camille Rantis, my co-witness to the bulldog.
- ❖ Daryl Rantis, whom no one will forget.

Jennifer's blog, www.LivingOnInk.com

Her fiction, www.TheMusketeerSeries.com

Humor yourself, jennysound.wordpress.com

Come Again Soon!

www.ingramcontent.com/pod-product-compliance
Lightning Source LLC
Chambersburg PA
CBHW030530010526
44110CB00048B/1068